Thomas John Capel

Confession and Absolution

Thomas John Capel

Confession and Absolution

ISBN/EAN: 9783337331344

Printed in Europe, USA, Canada, Australia, Japan

Cover: Foto ©Lupo / pixelio.de

More available books at **www.hansebooks.com**

Price, 25 Cents.

Confession

AND

Absolution

BY

Right Rev. Monsignor Capel, D.D.

Domestic Prelate of His Holiness, Leo XIII, happily reigning,
and Member of the Congregation of the Segnatura.

<hr>

"He hath placed in us the Ministry of Reconciliation."—2 Cor. V, 18.

<hr>

PHILADELPHIA:

PETER F. CUNNINGHAM & SON,

817 Arch Street.

1884.

Confession

—→ AND ←—

Absolution

BY

Right Reverend Monsignor Capel, D.D.

Domestic Prelate of His Holiness, Leo XIII, happily reigning, and
Member of the Congregation of the Segnatura.

"He hath placed in us the Ministry of Reconciliation."—2 Cor. v. 18.

—→✕←—

Philadelphia:

PETER F. CUNNINGHAM & SON,

No. 817 Arch Street.

—

1884

CONFESSION AND ABSOLUTION.

In the series of twenty-four conferences delivered in the Cathedral at Philadelphia, during this Lent, was one on "God's Conditions for Pardoning Sin." At the request of many, it is now published, but under the title of "Confession and Absolution." There have been made such modifications and additions as are necessitated by publication, and such others as will cover aspects of the question treated by me elsewhere in the United States.

The extracts from the Fathers which appear in the following pages are taken from the accurate and judicious collection known as "Faith of Catholics," a work in three volumes, well worthy the attention and study of those who, not having a library of the Fathers, or not conversant with the classical languages, are nevertheless anxious to know the evidence of the early Christian writers concerning the doctrines and practices of the Catholic Church.

T. J. CAPEL.

PHILADELPHIA:
Feast of Our Lady's Sorrows, 1884.

Confession and Absolution.

TEXT: "God hath reconciled us to Himself by Christ, and hath given to us the ministry of reconciliation. For God indeed was in Christ, reconciling the world to Himself, and He hath placed in us the word of reconciliation; we are therefore ambassadors for Christ."—2 Cor. v, 18.

NO more important question can be submitted for consideration to those who believe in the existence of God, in man's responsibility to his Creator, and in divine revelation, than what are God's conditions for pardoning sin. For however much men may doubt, deny, or dispute about religion, they can never impugn the fact that they are individually sinners. "If we say we have no sin, we deceive ourselves, and the truth is not in us;"[1] "in many things we all offend;"[2] even "the just man shall offend seven times."

Good sense, as well as faith, tells us that having willingly committed or consented to any thought, word, or deed prohibited by God, or having knowingly and wilfully omitted any duty imposed by the divine law, then have we revolted against our God. And should this be done with full knowledge and deliberation in a matter deemed grave by the Lawgiver, or grave in its own nature, or rendered so by circumstances, then has there been a grievous transgression of our duty to God.

The moment we so act, are we and our crime abominable in the sight of the All Holy. "Thou hatest all the workers of iniquity;"[4] and to the Lord "the wicked and his wickedness are hateful alike."[5] Our sin instantly merits eternal punish-

---

[1] 1 John i, 8. [2] James iii, 2. [3] Prov. xxiv, 16. [4] Ps. v, 6. [5] Wisd. xiv, 9.

ment: "If the just man turns himself away from his justice, and do iniquity according to all the abominations which the wicked man useth to work, shall he live? All his justices which he had done shall not be remembered."[1] "But the fearful, and unbelieving, and the abominable, and murderers, and whoremongers, and sorcerers, and idolaters, and all liars, they shall have their portion in the pool burning with fire and brimstone, which is the second death."[2] Finally, by our grievous sin do we destroy habitual or justifying grace, the supernatural life of the soul: "When concupiscence hath conceived, it bringeth forth sin; but sin, when it is completed, begetteth death."[3] Well, therefore, are we told: "Flee from sins as from the face of a serpent; for if thou comest near them, they will take hold of thee; the teeth thereof are the teeth of a lion, killing the souls of men."[4]

Deadly sin accordingly puts us at enmity with God, and deprives us of all claim on His justice. These are days when men talk much of their own rights. Little do they think to assert and uphold the rights of the King of Kings, the Lord of Lords. And so it escapes them that having violated their obligations to their Creator, their Redeemer, their Sanctifier, by grievous sin, they have no claim for pardon on the ground of justice; they can only appeal suppliantly to the infinite mercy and goodness of God for forgiveness. This being the case, the Almighty can and does impose His conditions for reconciling the sinner and for restoring the prodigal child to the lost sonship.

Of these conditions, one flows from the infinite holiness of His own nature, namely: contrition or repentance. The other, which is judicial absolution from sin, implying previous confession of it, is imposed by the revealed law of God, and is

---

[1] Ezech. xviii, 24. [2] Rev. xxi, 8. [3] James i, 15. [4] Ecclus. xxi, 2.

therefore a divine command obliging all—popes, bishops, priests, and people. Let us deal with these separately.

I.

Contrition or repentance does not mean a mere cessation from wrong-doing, and starting anew in the way of goodness, drowning in the past the evil done. On the contrary, as by sin we turned our backs on God to go into a far-off country, to spend there our substance, so by contrition must we turn again, retrace our steps, and journey to that Father and home whence we departed. Hence is the process named conversion to God, just as sin is defined to be an aversion from God. Moses, expressing this thought, says: "When thou shalt be touched with the repentance of thy heart, and return to Him, the Lord thy God will have mercy on thee."[1] And still more explicitly does the prophet Joel declare: "Be converted to Me with all your heart, in fasting, and in weeping, and in mourning; and rend your hearts, and not your garments, and turn to the Lord your God: for He is gracious and merciful, patient and rich in mercy."[2] Again, the inspired Word says: "Cast away from you all your transgressions, by which you have transgressed, and make to yourselves a new heart and a new spirit; and why will you die, O house of Israel?"[3]

The Lord God, whom we have outraged by sin, knows no past. "He is the God who is." In His holy sight, we who have sinned, and our transgressions, are ever abominable, unless we make to ourselves a new heart and a new spirit. "Be converted to Me, and I will be converted to thee," are the words of Him who exercises on us His great mercy.

Holy Church, in her General Council assembled at Trent, defined this contrition or repentance to be "a sorrow of mind,

---

[1] Deut. xxx, 1.   [2] Joel ii, 12.   [3] Ezech. xviii, 31.

and a detestation of sin committed, together with a determination of not sinning for the future"—"*animi dolor, ac detestatio de peccato commisso, cum proposito non peccandi de cætero.*" [1] And, as the Roman Catechism explains, this means no mere feeling, but a genuine act of the will. A mother may show more sensible signs of grief at the loss of her only child than when sorrowing for sin, yet this is not in the least inconsistent with the most perfect contrition or repentance.

There are times when the intense sorrow for sin arouses the whole being of man : exciting not only the higher, but also the lower and sensitive part of his nature. St. Mary Magdalen, David, and many other great penitents, wept bitter tears of sorrow for their past wrongs. This, though a heavenly favor, is no necessary part of repentance. Indeed, it is possible to weep and to have sensible sorrow without having a contrite heart. The three essential elements in contrition are : hatred of past sin, grief at having sinned, and a determined purpose at all costs to avoid, in the future, sin and the occasions of sin. These emanate from the will of man, not from his feeling ; they must be strong or intense enough to make the sinner prefer to endure any evil, or sacrifice any good, rather than again offend God, so infinitely good in Himself, and so infinitely good to man.

Unhappily, it is within our power to hate, to grieve, and to purpose amendment very sincerely, and yet not have that sorrow which fulfills God's condition 'for the pardon of sin. Some human motive—such as loss of health or wealth, injury to reputation and influence, the ignominy and servitude of wrong-doing—may lead a man to detestation of the past and to a firm resolve to avoid wrong in the future. Excellent as may be such a change of mind, yet it is not sufficient to obtain forgiveness from on high. It is based entirely on the injury and loss accruing

---

[1] Con. Trid. Sess. xiv, cap. 4.

to self. God is excluded from the whole idea; and yet it is against Him, and against Him alone, that we have sinned.

The sole sorrow acceptable to God is that which springs from a supernatural motive, the soul excited thereto by divine grace. In this is our utter helplessness shown; for while it is within our own power to do wrong, we cannot return to the path of duty and repent without the help of God. The remembrance of God's infinite love and perfections, accompanied by earnest. prayer for mercy, may rouse the soul to hatred and grief for its sin, and thus is generated that contrition perfect through charity for having offended so good a God, who is to be loved above all things, and this without regarding the consequences which sin brings on us. This sorrow, with the implicit or explicit desire to have recourse to the sacrament of penance, reconciles the soul at once with God, and restores the justifying or habitual grace lost by grievous sin. "There is no condemnation to those who are in Christ Jesus, who walk not after the flesh, but after the spirit." The soul about to go before God's judgment-seat, if it be in deadly sin, and have not at hand the means for obtaining absolution, is obliged to have this perfect contrition, or otherwise the sin remains unforgiven.

Again, the soul, contemplating in the sight of God the turpitude of sin, as made known to us by revelation, or the terror of God's judgment on those condemned to hell, or the irreparable loss of heaven consequent on sin, may be excited by fear of Him who hath power to cast into everlasting prison. The soul, awe-stricken by the painful sight of its own guilt, and by the sense of the judgment of God, yet hoping for pardon and resolved to sin no more, makes an initial act of the love of God, and appeals to His goodness for forgiveness. Though the motive is less perfect, yet "He who desireth not the death of the sinner, but that he be converted and live" does in His exceeding mercy accept this as sufficient for pardon, if there be added to it the actual reception of the sacrament of penance. In other words, in this case, unless the sinner shows himself to the authorized minister of reconciliation and receives his absolution, there is no pardon.

Whether this sorrow be of the perfect kind, arising purely from love of God, or whether it be less perfect, caused by fear of God: in either case, it is *internal*, seated in the mind and heart; it is *supernatural* in its motive, and springs from grace; it is *universal*, extending to every deadly sin committed; it is *sovereign*, displeasing the will more than any ill which could happen. This, then, is contrition: the first and necessary condition for the pardon of sin. It is begun and perfected in the soul by the impulse and by the assistance of the Holy Ghost. The grace of God, obtained through the precious blood of Jesus Christ, commences and completes the work of repentance.

II.

It has pleased God, as we learn by the Christian revelation, to institute a human and visible Ministry of Reconciliation for sinners. St. Paul expresses this in the clearest way, writing to the Corinthians: "God hath reconciled us to Himself by Christ, and hath given to us the ministry of reconciliation. For God indeed was in Christ, reconciling the world to Himself, and He hath placed in us the word of reconciliation; we are therefore ambassadors for Christ." In this passage does the Apostle teach the truth declared elsewhere: "Christ died for our sins, the just for the unjust, that He might offer us to God, being put to death indeed in the flesh."[1] Herein is it taught very plainly that we are redeemed by Jesus, and that there is no other name under heaven given to men whereby they must be saved. He

---

[1] 1 Pet. iii, 18.

alone paid the price of our redemption; by His precious blood alone are we redeemed; and through Him alone is sin forgiven.

But, in the same passage, St. Paul is equally explicit in declaring: "He hath given to us"—namely, the Apostles—"the ministry of reconciliation." [1] In this there is no pretension that the Apostles were the reconcilers by inherent right; theirs is an agency of reconciliation, and hence does St. Paul speak of them as ambassadors of Christ. What is here so positively asserted by the Apostle was very definitely instituted by our Lord, as is recounted in the Gospels.

To the Apostles and their successors did Jesus Christ impart the power to baptize all nations. By baptism is man purified from original sin, and made a child of God. The efficient cause of such pardon of original sin is Jesus Christ; and yet it is by a Minister of Reconciliation, pouring water and saying the words "I baptize thee in the name of the Father," etc., etc., that the cleansing is effected. It is passing strange that those who believe in baptism as the appointed means whereby a minister reconciles a soul in original sin should hesitate to admit the ministerial power of forgiving actual sin. The principle is the same.

For, in like manner, on the day of the resurrection, Jesus Christ appeared to the eleven, whom He had made priests at the Last Supper, and said: "Peace be to you. As the Father hath sent me, I also send you. When He had said this, He breathed on them, and He said to them: Receive ye the Holy Ghost; whose sins you shall forgive, they are forgiven them; and whose sins you shall retain, they are retained." [2]

The passage is exceptionally clear. Our Lord, who is possessed of all power in heaven and on earth, makes his Apostles participate in the power of forgiving sin. They derive it from Him, and receive it by the in-breathing of the Holy Spirit. It

---

[1] 2 Cor. v, 18.   [2] John xx, 21.

is no product of their learning, or experience, or piety, nor is it any right inborn in them; but it is a divine gift, given by the Redeemer to His ministers for the sanctification of souls. By it are His legitimate ministers made co-operators in the work of reconciliation. Already had the Scribes thought that Jesus blasphemed when He said to the man sick of the palsy: "Son, be of good heart: thy sin is forgiven thee." To convince them that the Son *of man* hath power to forgive sin, Jesus healed the man of the palsy. The multitude, seeing this, feared and glorified God, who had given such power *to men.*[1] The power is of God, who alone can forgive sin, though He exercises it through men as channels of His grace. The power of working miracles in like manner belongs to God's omnipotence; yet did He condescend to allow His apostles and others to share in it. In this they were but His agents.

The passage, in the next place, expresses judicial power: for the commission draws the distinction between remitting sin and retaining sin. This exercise of discretionary power does not depend on the arbitrary will of the Apostles, but has to be decided according to the Gospel law of true repentance described previously. The Apostles are appointed ministerial judges of the matter on which they are to pronounce sentence of remission or of retention, and their sentence is effective, being ratified by God.

Now, it is a primary condition of just judgment that the judge should not only be cognizant of the law which is to be administered, but also of the cause submitted for judgment. Applying this to the exercise of the judicial power with which the Apostles are invested, two things are needed: the first, that they should know the law and the conditions on which sin was to be retained or remitted. This they could only learn of God. The second, that they should know the sin committed, its nature

---

[1] Matt. ix, 2.

and its circumstances. But sin is in the soul. Who then but the individual offender can know the sins for which forgiveness is sought? And the disclosure can only come from the wrong-doer. Clearly then, confession, in the ordinary course of things, is the necessary and preliminary condition for seeking absolution from sin. Whether this confession be made in public or in private is a mere matter of convenience, to be decided by those who absolve. The honest humble accusation of all deadly sins constitutes the essential character of such confession or avowal of transgressions.

That interior contrition is to be followed by the judicial sentence of a duly-appointed priest, to whom confession of all deadly sins has been previously made, is the unanimous teaching of the Christian writers from the earliest date. The existence of Penance as the Sacrament of Reconciliation, at all times in the Church, is permanent evidence to the belief and practice of early Christians.

Among the living Greek communions are to be found descendants of those sects which either separated from or were cast off by the Church centuries ago. The Photians date back to the tenth century; the Nestorians, the Jacobites, the Abyssinians, the Copts, to the fifth and sixth centuries. Differing as these do in sundry points of doctrine, yet on the matter of absolution and confession they have the same teaching and practice. It is no question of unburdening a troubled conscience for peace and counsel, but confession is exacted as a necessary condition for obtaining pardon. In 1576, the patriarch Jeremias of Constantinople sent to the Protestant theologians of Tübingen a declaration of the belief of the Greeks. In it, among other doctrines, that of the absolute necessity of detailed confession to a priest is asserted. These sects then are, by their practice and teaching, witnesses to the truth concerning the sacrament of reconciliation as taught by Holy Church in our day.

Early heresies contribute, in like manner, their part to the mass of irrefragable evidence in support of the doctrine. As early as the second century, Eusebius says A. D. 171, the Montanists arose in Asia Minor. Among other things, Montanus, their founder, taught that were any to "commit grievous sin after baptism, to deny Christ, or have been stained with the guilt of impurity, murder, or like crimes, they were to be for ever cut off from the communion of the Church." While admitting that power to forgive sin was given by Christ to the Apostles and their successors, Montanus wished to restrict that power, excluding from its domain idolatry, impurity, and homicide.

Some eighty years later, two schisms arose: one in North Africa, led by the priest Novatus, aided by the deacon Felicissimus, the other by the anti-pope Novatian, in Rome. Both were prompted by the question of receiving into the communion of the Church those who had lapsed into idolatry, or had denied the faith during the times of persecution. The African schism insisted on the laxest possible line of action, namely, to receive indiscriminately without proof of penitence. The schism in Rome pursued the most unyielding rigorism. "Whoever," said Novatian, its leader, "has offered sacrifice to idols, or stained his soul with the guilt of sin, can no longer remain within the Church; and if he be of those who have denied the faith, he can not again enter her communion: for her members consist only of pure and faithful souls."

These contentions had one great advantage: they brought into prominence the teaching of the Church concerning "the forgiveness of sin," and occasioned a more scientific and dogmatic statement of the doctrine of penance. In the controversy, figure the names of the Pope Cornelius, of St. Cyprian, of St. Athanasius, of St. Pacian, of St. Gregory Nazianzen, of Tertullian. Until the schismatics were driven to extremities, it is plain both sides took it for granted that the ministry of reconciliation was given to the Church by Jesus Christ, and that the exercise of the ministry consisted in pronouncing judicial sentence of pardon on those who had shown repentance and had confessed their grievous sins. Religious strife in this case produces the interesting evidence that, as early as the second and third centuries, Confession and Absolution were held and practiced as necessary for the pardoning of sin under the Christian dispensation.

We may now turn to the writings of the Fathers of the first five centuries. It will be seen that throughout, when treating of the forgiveness of sin, it is always assumed that the priests of Holy Church were endowed with and exercised the power of absolution on those who had sinned after baptism. The sacrament of pardon is constantly referred to under different names: penance, confession, absolution, exomologesis, reconciliation, the second baptism, the laborious baptism, the second plank after the shipwreck. Of these, exomologesis occurs very frequently. Its meaning varies: at one time it signifies manifestation of sin, whether in private or in public; and at another it expresses the public penance and confession in vogue in the first ages of the Church.

At the end of the first century, St. Clement of Rome— whom St. Paul, in his Epistle to the Philippians, numbers among " his fellow-laborers whose names are in the book of life"— writes, in the Second Epistle ascribed to him and addressed to the Corinthians : "As long as we are in this world, let us repent with our whole heart of the evil deeds which we have done in the flesh, that we may be saved by the Lord whilst we have time for repentance. For after that we have gone forth from this world, we are no longer able *to confess* or repent there."[1]

---

[1] Ep. ii, ad Cor. n. 8.

In the middle of the second century, appeared the "Teaching of the Twelve Apostles," now causing no small attention in the religious world. Its date is variously stated from 120 to 160 A.D. To it does St. Clement of Alexandria, who lived into the second decade of the third century, make reference. The text, together with a translation, is now published. Therein (Chap. IV) do we read: "Thou shalt by no means forsake the Lord's commandments, but shalt guard what thou hast received, neither adding thereto nor taking therefrom. In the Church thou shalt *confess thy transgressions*, and thou shalt not come forward for thy prayer with an evil conscience." And again (Chap. XIV): "But on the Lord's Day do ye assemble and break bread, and give thanks, after *confessing your transgressions*, that your sacrifice may be pure."

In the latter part of the second century, St. Irenæus, Bishop of Lyons, writing against the Valentinians and certain Gnostics led by Marcus, states explicitly that many of the women who had been led into heresy and impurity, and who afterwards returned to the Church, *confessed even publicly*, and wept over their defilement. "But others, ashamed to do this, and in some manner secretly despairing within themselves of the life of God, apostatized entirely."[1]

The same writer mentions that "Cordon who appeared before Marcion, he also under Hyginus, the eighth bishop, having come into the Church *and confessing*, thus completed his career."

In the last decade of the second century, and in the first twenty years of the third century, the famed Tertullian, who was born at Carthage, and who lived and labored in Rome and North Africa, wrote, before joining the Montanist sect: "If thou drawest back from confession (exomologesis), consider in

---

[1] Adv. Hæres. l. i. cxiii, n. 4, 5, 6, 7.

thine heart that hell-fire which confession shall quench for thee; and first imagine to thyself the greatness of the punishment, that thou mayest not doubt concerning the adoption of the remedy. * * * When, therefore, thou knowest that against hell-fire, after that first protection of the baptism ordained by the Lord, there *is* yet in confession (exomologesis) a second aid, why dost thou abandon thy salvation? Why delay to enter on that which thou knowest will heal thee? Even dumb and unreasoning creatures know at the season the medicines which are given them from God. * * * Shall the sinner, *knowing that confession has been instituted by the Lord* for his restoration, pass over that which restored the king of Babylon to his kingdom? * * * Why should I say more of these two planks, I may call them, for saving men?"[1]

In the middle of the third century, Origen labored at Alexandria, in Egypt, and later at Cæsarea, in Palestine. Again and again does he make reference to confession of sin and its absolution by a priest. "Hear therefore now," says he, "how many are the remissions of sin in the Gospels. The first is this by which we are baptized unto the remission of sins. * * * There is also yet a seventh, although hard and laborious: the remission of sins through penitence when the sinner washeth his bed with tears, and his tears become his bread day and night, and when he is not *ashamed to declare his sin to the priest of the Lord, and seek a remedy.*"[2] And commenting on the words of the Psalmist—"Because I declare my iniquity"—Origen writes: "Wherefore see what divine Scripture teaches us, that we must not hide sin within us. * * * But if a man become his own accuser, while he accuses himself and confesses, he at the same time ejects the sin, and digests the whole cause of the disease. Only look diligently round to whom thou oughtest *to confess*

---

[1] De Pænit. n. 8–12. [2] Hom. in Levit. n. 4.

thy sin. Prove first the physician, * * * that so in fine thou mayest do and follow whatever he shall have said, whatever counsel he shall have given."[1] Again does Origen write: "For if we have done this, and revealed our sins not only to God, but also to *those who are able to heal our wounds and sins,* our sins will be blotted out by Him who saith: 'Behold, I will blot out thy iniquities as a cloud, and thy sins as a mist.'"[2]

In the first half of the fourth century, flourished St. Cyprian, Bishop of Carthage. He repeatedly refers to the practice of confession and absolution. The following passage from his work "De Lapsis" will suffice to show his mind: "God perceives the things that are hidden, and considers those that are hidden and concealed. None can escape the eye of God: He sees the heart and breast of every person, and He will judge not only our actions, but also our words and thoughts. He regards the minds of all, and the wishes conceived in the hidden recesses of the breast. In fine, how much loftier in faith and in fear (of God) superior are they who, though implicated in no crime of sacrifice, or of accepting a certificate, yet because they have only had thought thereof, this very thing *sorrowingly and honestly confessing before the priests of God, make a confession* (*exomologesis*) *of their conscience,* expose the burthen of the soul, seek out a salutary cure even for light and little wounds, knowing that it is written 'God will not be mocked.'"

In the early part of the fourth century, Lactantius writes: "As every sect of heretics thinks its followers are above all other Christians, and its own the Catholic Church, it is to be known that is the true Catholic Church wherein *is confession and penitence* which wholesomely heals the wounds and sins to which the weakness of the flesh is subject."[3]

In the first quarter of the fourth century, Eusebius, the

[1] In Ps. xxxvii, n. 6.   [2] Hom. xvii in Lucam.   [3] Divin. Inst. l. iv, c. 30.

well-known ecclesiastical historian and Bishop of Cæsarea, leaves
on record, that the Emperor Philip, who wished to join in the
prayers of the Church, was not permitted to do so "until he
made his exomologesis (confession), and classed himself with
those who were separated on account of their sins."[1]

In the same century, St. Hiliary of Poictiers writes: "There
is the most powerful and most useful medicine for the diseases
of deadly vices in their confession. * * * Confession of sin is
this, that what has been done by thee thou confess to be a sin,
through thy conviction that it is sin."[2]

In the fourth century, St. Athanasius, whose name is iden-
tified with the General Council of Nice, is equally explicit. "As
man," says he, "is illuminated with the grace of the Holy Spirit
by the priest that baptizes, so also *he who confesses in penitence
receives through the priest*, by the grace of Christ, the remission
of sin."

In this same century, St. Pacian writes: "'But you will
say you forgive sin to the penitent, whereas in baptism alone it
is allowed you to loose sin.' Not to me at all, but to God only,
who both in baptism forgives the guilt incurred, and rejects not
the tears of the penitent. But what I do, I do not by my own
right, but by the Lord's. * * * Wherefore, whether we baptize,
whether we constrain to penitence, or *grant pardon to the penitent*, Christ is our authority. It is for you to see to it, whether
Christ hath this power, whether Christ have done this."[3]

In the same century, St. Ambrose, disciple of Origen, writes:
"Sins are remitted by the word of God, of which the Levite is
the interpreter and also the executor; they are also remitted by
the *office of the priest and the sacred ministry*."[4]

Writer after writer continues in the same strain, in this and
the following century. The passages cited clearly indicate that

---

[1] Hist. Ecc. Bk. vi, c. 34. [2] Tract. in Ps. cxxxviii. [3] Ep. iii, n. 7-9. [4] De
Cain et Abel, l. 2, c. 4.

confession and absolution are assumed to be the ordinary channel whereby sin is pardoned. Throughout they, as the Fathers of the preceding centuries, make the true dispenser of forgiveness God in general, or, at other times, Jesus Christ, or again, the Holy Spirit; but they are equally explicit in declaring the earthly visible organ whereby the pardon is exercised to be the Bishop, the Priest, the Ministers of the Church. These Christian writers constantly prove the Ministry of Reconciliation by reference to the passages concerning loosing and binding, in the eighteenth chapter of St. Matthew, and forgiving and retaining sin, in the twentieth chapter of St. John.

The great St. Jerome writes: "In the same way, therefore, that *there* (among the Jews) the priests make the leper clean or unclean, so also here (in the Church) does the bishop or priest bind and loose not those who are innocent or guilty, but, according to his office, after *hearing the various kinds of sins,* he knows who is to be bound and who loosed." [1]

And, in similar strain, does St. John Chrysostom comment on the words "Whatsoever ye shall bind on earth," etc., etc.: " * * * this bond touches the very soul itself, and reaches even unto heaven; and *what the priests shall do below,* the same does God ratify above, and the Lord confirms the sentence of his servants." [2]

And St. Augustine: "For this end are sins signified by these curtains, that they may be *expressed by confession,* and may, by the grace which *is given to the Church, be abolished.*" [3]

The authors we have cited, and in whose writings many other passages are to be found, are representatives during the first five centuries of the Church in North Africa, in Egypt, in Asia Minor, in Greece, in Italy, in Gaul. They are unanimous in upholding the power of absolution and the necessity of confession.

---

[1] Com. in Matt. c. xviii. [2] Vol. I, Lib. iii, n. 5, de Sacerd. [3] In Exod. n. cviii.

But a most unexpected witness is to be found in one of the great Protestant communions. The English Government, under the Tudor dynasty, threw off its allegiance in things ecclesiastical to the Holy See. The sovereigns of England then claimed that spiritual authority heretofore exercised by the Pope. Henceforth, the Church was not *in*, but *of* England. It became a State Department, the archbishops and bishops receiving their appointment, care of souls, and jurisdiction, from the king, just as the judges, the officers of the army and navy, are commissioned to their circuits, their regiments, and their ships. *The Crown is* not only the fountain-head of all spiritual governing-power, but the Crown, aided later by its Council, became the final Court of Appeal in all disputes about doctrine.

The Established communion, among other matters, holds in its Thirty-nine Articles that "Penance is not a sacrament of the Gospel." And in the Book of Homilies, which the said Articles commend as containing "good and wholesome doctrine," do we read: "We ought to acknowledge none other priest for deliverance from our sins but Jesus Christ. * * * It is most evident and plain that this auricular confession hath not the warrant of God's word. * * * I do not say but that, if any do find themselves troubled in conscience, they may repair to their learned curate or pastor, *or to some other godly learned man,* and show the trouble and doubt of their conscience to them, that they may receive at their hand the comfortable salve of God's word; but it is against the true Christian liberty that any man should be bound to the numbering of his sins, as it hath been used heretofore in the time of blindness and ignorance."[1] It is clear that both the Articles and the Book of Homilies deny the power of absolution and the necessity of confession as essential conditions, in the ordinary course of things, for the forgiveness of sin.

---

[1] Homily on Repentance, part ii.

The Book of Common Prayer—the Liturgy of the Anglican communion—in the office for visiting the sick, does urge the confession of the sick person, and gives the form of absolution to be used by the minister. In the Book of Common Prayer used by the Episcopalians in the United States, this direction concerning confession and absolution is omitted.

The result of the teaching of the Articles was the complete destruction, in the mind of the people of England, during three centuries, of the need of confession and absolution. And, until some fifty years ago, it was unknown for Anglicans to go to confession. A change came, and certain of the clergy of the Established communion began to teach the necessity of confession. This produced open revolt in their camp; the matter became so serious that the Convocation sitting in 1873 gave it consideration, and the Bishop of Salisbury boldly said: "Habitual confession is unholy, illegal, and full of mischief." The Bishop of Lichfield, in indignation, declared: "I would rather resign my office than hold it, if it was supposed that I was giving young men the right to practice habitual confession." The Archbishop of Canterbury said: "I am ready to revoke the license of any curate charged with hearing confessions." And Doctor Brown, Bishop of Ely, declared: "In no other communion would it be possible for a man to set himself up as the general confessor of a district, without any other authority than his own."

The assembled bishops published a formal document, wherein they declare: "The Church of England, in the Twenty-fifth Article, affirms that penance is not to be counted for a sacrament of the Gospel, and, as judged by her formularies, knows no such words as Sacramental Confession." And in this same declaration, commenting on the two instances wherein the Book of Common Prayer recommends seeking the aid of a clergyman, is it said: "This special provision, however, does not authorize the ministers

of the Church to require, of any who may resort to them to
open their grief, a particular or detailed enumeration of their
sins; or to require private confession previous to receiving the
holy communion ; or to enjoin, or even encourage, any practice
of habitual confession to a priest; or to teach that such practice
of habitual confession, or the being subject to what has been
termed the direction of a priest, is a condition of attaining to
the highest spiritual life."

Notwithstanding these clear utterances in Convocation, young
curates and vicars took to themselves authority, and began to
hear confession and pronounce absolution. These gentlemen had
never been prepared for the work: they had to obtain their
knowledge from the manuals in use among Catholic priests.
Their bishops could give them no authority; and so these
clergymen became an authority to themselves, and declared they
had power to forgive sin, merely because they were ordained
priests. This pretension could not be made by any priest or
bishop of the Catholic Church, however valid might be his
orders. To the sacramental power of orders must be added
juridical authority to absolve.

Such was the movement in England. I find it transported
to the United States. And.I am told by honorable trustworthy
people that in Boston, New York, Baltimore, Philadelphia, and
other cities, there are Episcopalian clergymen who insist that
their penitents shall confess at regular intervals. That such a
fact is possible, or that persons should be found ready to submit
themselves to such a self-asserted *ministry*, notwithstanding the
clear declaration of the Thirty-nine Articles, tho official com-
mentary of the Book of Homilies cited above, and the formal
condemnation of the English bishops, is simply incredible.

In the United States it is the more inexplicable, inasmuch
as by the Declaration of Independence there could be no jurisdic-

tion derived from the Crown of England. And, consequently, the Episcopal Church, formed as it was after the Independence, could not, from the nature of the case, receive jurisdiction from without. It formed itself into a corporation, and its only authority was generated by itself. But that of confessing and absolving from sin could not have been so created: no more than it could have been done by the Episcopal Methodist, the Presbyterian, the Quaker, or any other religious corporation. It is not unreasonable in a matter so grave, affecting the eternal salvation of men, to ask of these gentlemen, calling themselves Reverend Father Confessors, who gives them approbation and authority to pass the judicial sentence of pardon. Assuredly, their bishops do not, and cannot. Excellent and beyond reproach as are these clergymen, well-instructed as they may be in the casuistry of the Roman Catholic moral theological works, their absolutions are null and void, and of no more avail than if pronounced by mere laymen.

Apart from this, how has such a change been wrought in the minds of Episcopalians on both sides of the Atlantic? The Oxford movement of some forty-five years ago turned men's minds to the early history of the Church: and, finding confession and absolution then to be the ordinary and necessary conditions for reconciliation with God, the practice was introduced, but without seeing the important truth that, over and above valid ordination, there is needed jurisdiction from the Church, so as to make absolution of avail.

This new school of religious opinion in the Episcopal communion contributes its share of evidence in upholding what the Church of God has always taught, viz: that over and above having a genuine supernatural sorrow for sin, there is ordinarily required on the part of the sinner confession of sin, followed by the judicial absolution of God's minister, approved and authorized

by the Church, who alone possesses the power of the keys to
remit or retain sin.

The belief and practice of the earliest schismatics, the
statements of the Fathers—representatives of all Christian lands
in the first five centuries, and the discovery made by High
Churchmen in our day, render separately and cumulatively
evidence to the belief in "Confession and Absolution" which
no reasonable man can or ought to reject.

Well, therefore, did the Church, assembled in General
Council at Trent, sum up the question: "It is certain that,
in the Church, nothing else is required of penitents but that,
after each has examined himself diligently, and searched all the
folds and recesses of his conscience, he confess those sins by
which he shall remember that he has mortally offended his Lord
and God; whilst the other sins, which do not occur to him after
diligent thought, are understood to be included, as a whole, in
that same confession; for which sins we confidently say with
the prophet: 'From my secret sins cleanse me, O Lord.' Now,
the difficulty of a confession like this, and the shame of making
known one's sins, might indeed seem a grievous thing, were it
not alleviated by the so many and so great advantages and
consolations which are most assuredly bestowed by absolution
upon all who worthily approach to this sacrament. For the rest,
as to the manner of confessing secretly to a priest alone, although
Christ has not forbidden that a person may, in punishment of his
sins, and for his own humiliation, as well for an example to others
for the edification of the Church that has been scandalized,
confess his sins publicly, nevertheless, this is not commanded by
a divine precept; neither would it be very prudent to enjoin, by
any human law, that sins, especially such as are secret, should be
made known by a public confession. Wherefore, whereas the
secret sacramental confession, which was in use from the begin-

ning in Holy Church, and is still also in use, has always been commended by the most holy Fathers with a great and unanimous consent, the vain calumny of those is manifestly refuted who are not ashamed to teach that confession is alien from the divine command and is a human invention." [1]

III.

So far, the doctrine concerning God's conditions for reconciling the sinner with God has been limited to the interior supernatural repentance, together with absolution and confession. The other element—satisfaction—which is not of the essence of contrition, but perfects it, has not been treated, simply because in another conference it is intended to deal with this question in connection with the works of penance and the doctrine of indulgences.

Before closing the question now under consideration, it is right that certain objections, urged oftentimes in good faith, should be duly met.

It is, as was said elsewhere, by no inherent power that the Apostles and their successors are able to remit sin. God, and God alone, can do so, though He can delegate this to others. This He has done. But to secure so transcendent an authority from abuse, two elements are necessary before it can be exercised.

First, from God, and through the appointed sacrament, must man be constituted a priest—that is, an offerer of sacrifice. This comes direct from God, and is called the power of Order, and is obtained by ordination. This was given to the Apostles at the Last Supper, when our Lord said: "Do this in commemoration of me." After His resurrection, there was given the power or capability to forgive sin, by the words "Receive ye the Holy Ghost: whose sins you shall forgive, they are forgiven; and whose sins you shall retain, they are retained."

---

[1] Con. Trent, Sess. xiv, cap. 5.

The second element comes also from.God, but indirectly, as it reaches the individual minister through the Church. It is the authority or commission of the Church to a priest or bishop to exercise the power of pardoning which he has received of God. This is called jurisdiction. It is included in the words said to Peter: "To thee will I give the keys of the kingdom of heaven; whatsoever thou shalt bind on earth shall be bound also in heaven, and whatsoever thou shalt loose on earth shall be loosed also in heaven."[1] Many a man has all the innate and acquired talent to be an excellent judge, a proficient ambassador, an efficient naval or military officer; but over and above capability there is needed commission or appointment by competent authority. So, in like manner, bishops and priests possess the power to pardon, but jurisdiction is needed to say on whom and where this power is to be exercised. Merely because a man is ordained validly, this does not give him the power to absolve; without jurisdiction—or, as it is technically called, "faculties"— his absolution has no more value than would that of a layman.

It will be evident that as jurisdiction comes from God but through the Church, she can control those who are to exercise the power of pardoning sin; hence, she insists that her priests shall carefully study the moral law, just as a lawyer does civil law. She exacts that those who hear confessions shall, by examination, prove their competency in the way of knowledge. She trains from boyhood her Levites to the sacred work they have to do, and she permits only those to be admitted to the Ministry of Reconciliation whose piety, past conduct, and judgment commend them for confessions. And even when the jurisdiction is given, it is restricted as to time, persons, place, and may be withdrawn if deemed advisable.

Thus, then, is every care taken in the selection and in the

---

[1] Matt. xvi, 19, and xviii, 18.

preparation of priests for the work of hearing confessions and absolving from sin. Even after they are duly appointed, the restriction of the power to time, places, persons, and causes, together with the varied tests of competency and the opportunities for increased knowledge, constitute a solid control in the wielding of such power. Then the priest's own belief and conscience, as well as the obligation to confess his sins and seek absolution for them, add to the faithful exercise of his duties as confessor.

But, over and above all these human precautions and considerations, the very fact that God instituted the Tribunal of Penance as the usual channel for pardoning sin obliges us to realize that He himself would protect the administration of the sacrament.

Medical men and lawyers are not trained and selected for their profession as are priests, nor are they aided in their duties by special divine protection. Yet relying on them as gentlemen and on their professional honor, clients, without fear or suspicion, entrust to these themselves and their affairs.

Why then not concede to priests at least this same measure of honorability? They, like doctors and lawyers, must for their work be theoretically cognizant of the crimes, iniquities, and weaknesses of mankind. But they, no more than doctors or lawyers, speak of these things, unless the penitent has been guilty of and confesses some such offence.

Again, let it be remembered that it is not as in a court of justice, where the plea of "not guilty" is set up, and all has then to be wormed out by examination in the most detailed manner. For the penitent enters the confessional as self-accuser, states the offence, together with the number of times it has happened, and any circumstances which may alter or aggravate the deed. There are, therefore, in confession, none of the nauseous details and descriptions of crime which may be heard in our courts and read in our newspapers.

Good sense ought to make objectors remember that priests have mothers and sisters and relations whom they love; and priests would be the first to prevent these beloved ones from the corrupting influences which enemies ignorantly attribute to the confessional.

Once more let it be remembered that the Tribunal of Penance is for the accusation and absolution of sin. Name, nor abode, nor fortune, nor domestic concerns, have any place there. The priest is the spiritual physician, and it is the disease which is submitted to him; all else is foreign to his office, nor has he right to ask of other matters. Nay, more: a sacramental secret surrounds his work; this involves obligations greater than any natural or promised secrecy. Information obtained in confession the priest can never use, be it in his own interest, or in that of a family, or of the State, or even of the Church. Therefore, to imagine the Tribunal of Penance to be an engine for obtaining and using information in domestic concerns and family secrets, is to be sorely ignorant of the duties and obligations of a confessor.

Objectors of another kind urge that confession induces persons to sin more readily, or at least transfers the keeping of conscience to the priest.

Seeing that all which is demanded by Protestants for repentance must be in the mind of the Catholic before he can be absolved, it is clear the objection raised is futile and has no foundation. Of course, for those who believe that Catholics obtain pardon by payment of money, the objection would have weight. But it can hardly be imagined that in the nineteenth century, among an intelligent people like Americans, there are to be found persons believing Catholics so bereft of reason as to believe sin can be so forgiven.

On the other hand, and quite apart from the humiliation of confession, its practice augments the fear of returning to wallow in the mire of sin.

Nowhere is the soul of man more prone to self-deception than in the matter of true repentance. Temptation may cease, and with it comes cessation of wrong-doing. This may, under self-deception, be easily construed into conversion. Self-interest and passion may so blind a man that he may imagine himself truly repentant, notwithstanding that he has not pardoned injuries, or reconciled himself to enemies, or restored ill-gotten goods, or retracted calumny, or compensated for wrongs inflicted, or is not disposed to avoid occasions of sin, and the like.

The confessor has to intervene, remind the penitent of these duties, and they shall be done, before he can absolve from sin. Here, instead of becoming the keeper of the sinner's conscience, the confessor is but the instructor: duty and responsibility remain in all their extent to the penitent. And the penitent has to test the genuineness of his contrition by unmistakable obligations to be complied with, if forgiveness of sin is to be obtained.

To have a wise prudent spiritual adviser, to have an experienced physician of the soul, to have a merciful but strict judge of moral duty, is to have the greatest moral support on earth, even apart from the superadded sacramental character of such an officer. It is this blessed gift which the Catholic has in his legitimately-approved and authorized confessor.

Prejudice or ignorance can alone construe such an inestimable treasure into "making the priest the keeper of a man's conscience, and the destroyer of man's spiritual liberty and of his responsibility to his Creator."

How different are the opinions of thoughtful men, concerning this Tribunal of Penance, will be seen from the following: One is a Frenchman, who, unhappily, apostatized from the Catholic Church; the second is a German philosopher, who lived and died a Protestant; the third is one of the profoundest thinkers of our day, who, born in the Episcopal Church in England, served her some forty years, and then left her to enter the Catholic, Apostolic, and Roman Church.

The first of these—Voltaire—thus writes:

"The enemies of the Roman Church, who have assailed the salutary institution of confession, appear to have removed the strongest restraint which can be put upon secret crimes. The sages of antiquity themselves felt the importance of it." [1]

The second—Leibnitz—in his "System of Theology," says:

"The Institution of sacramental confession is assuredly worthy of the divine wisdom, and, of all the doctrines of religion, it is the most admirable and the most beautiful. It was admired by the Chinese and the inhabitants of Japan. The necessity of confessing sin is sufficient to preserve from it those who still preserve their modesty; and yet, if any fail, confession consoles and restores them. I look on a grave and prudent confessor as a great instrument of God for the salvation of souls. His counsels regulate the sentiments, reprove vices, remove occasions of sin, cause the restitution of ill-acquired property, and the reparation of wrongs; clear up doubts, console under afflictions—in fine, cure or relieve all the evils of the soul; and as nothing in the world is more precious than a faithful friend, what is the value of that friend when he is bound by his functions and fitted by his knowledge to devote to you all his care, under the seal of the most inviolable secrecy?"

The third of these writers — Cardinal Newman — thus expresses himself:

"How many are the souls in distress, anxiety, or loneliness,

---

[1] Annales de l'Empire, vol. i, p. 41.

whose one need is to find a being to whom they can pour out
their feelings unheard by the world. Tell them out they must.
They cannot tell them out to those whom they see every hour;
they want to tell them, and not to them. And they want to tell
them out, yet be as if they be not told; they wish to tell
them to one who is strong enough to bear them, yet not too
strong to despise them; they wish to tell them to one who can
at once advise and sympathize with them; they wish to relieve
themselves of a load to gain a solace: to receive the assurance
that there is one who thinks of them, and one to whom in
thought they can recur; to whom they can betake themselves,
if necessary, from time to time, while they are in the world.
How many a Protestant's heart would leap at the news of such
a benefit, putting aside all ideas of sacramental ordinance, or of
a grant of pardon, and the conveyance of grace! If there is
a heavenly idea in the Catholic Church, looking at it simply as
an idea—surely, next after the Blessed Sacrament, confession is
such.   And such is it ever found, in fact; the very act of
kneeling, the low and contrite voice, the sign of the cross—
hanging, so to say, over the head bowed low—and the words of
peace and blessing. Oh, what a soothing charm is there which
the world can neither give nor take away! Oh, what piercing
heart-subduing tranquility, provoking tears of joy, is poured
almost substantially and physically upon the soul—the oil of
gladness, as Scripture calls it—when the penitent at length rises,
his God reconciled to him, his sins rolled away for ever! This
is confession as it is in fact, as those bear witness to it who know
it by experience."[1]

---

[1] Card. Newman, Apg. Diff. p. 351.

FINIS.